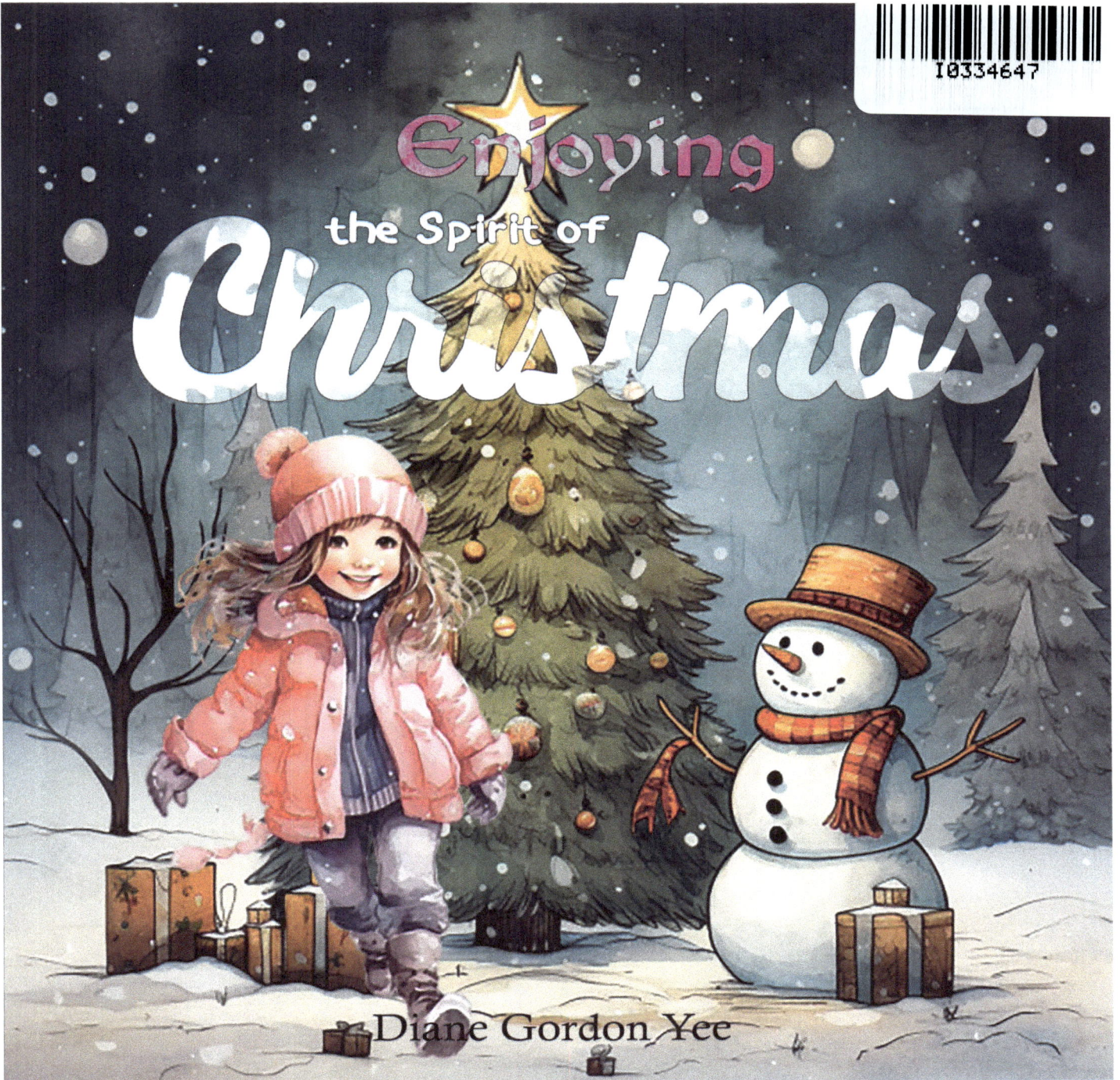

When Noella went to her gramma's house she was still not happy.

She had a scowl on her face.

Her gramma noticed and asked why she was upset.

She said she didn't like Christmas.

Her gramma smiled and asked her to go for a walk with her.

She suggested that she would feel better if she did.

Noella was reluctant to go but she said yes because she loved her gramma.

Her gramma laughed and said 'cold' is not a description but a feeling.

Then her gramma smiled and asked what season it was.

Noella said **"WINTER"** without hesitation.

Noella's gramma then said

"Look around you. It looks beautiful and peaceful. It looks like a **WONDERLAND**."

Noella was again confused as she looked around.

Her gramma grabbed her hand, squeezed it
and repeated again, "Look around.
It looks like a winter wonderland."
She hugged her and said,
"that's the name of the song."

WINTER WONDERLAND.

Have you heard of that song?
Do you know the words?

WINTER WONDERLAND

Sleigh bells ring, are you listening?
In the lane, snow is glistening
A beautiful sight, we're happy tonight
Walking in a Winter Wonderland!
Gone away is the bluebird,
Here to stay is a new bird.
He sings a love song as we go along,
Walking in a Winter Wonderland!
In the meadow we can build a snowman,
Then pretend that he is Parson Brown.
He'll say "Are you married?"
We'll say "No man!
But you can do the job when you're in town".
Later on, we'll conspire
As we dream by the fire,
To face unafraid, the plans that we've made,
Walking in a Winter Wonderland!

Noella laughed and said "Oh, you're right. How cool!
It does look really nice."

Her gramma put her hand under Noella's chin and
gently pushed it upwards towards her so that they were
eye to eye and then quietly said

"Christmas is not about presents and toys.
It's about the joy of what is
around you; snow, trees, lights.
It is also the feeling of happiness and joy
of being with someone you love and being
in a place of beauty."

Her gramma then gave her a kiss on the tip of her nose
and they started to walk some more in silence enjoying
the **SPIRIT** of the holidays in their very own
WINTER WONDERLAND.

As they got closer to the center of town,
Noella heard the voices of other children
and the lyrics of Christmas music.
Her smile widened. She felt happier and
was truly enjoying her time outside with her gramma.
Noella and her gramma walked towards
the children who were busily making a snowman.

Do you like making snowmen?

Noella and her gramma both noticed them at the same time and smiled at each other.

They both stopped and watched.

They saw a daddy putting up Christmas lights and two children happily watching their mommy try to hang some baubles.

Their smiles grew bigger as they watched the family decorate their house with garland.

**Do you know
what baubles and garland are?**

The family seemed to be laughing and having
a good time with each other.

Noella's gramma looked at her and
simply said they were
**"ENJOYING the SPIRIT of
CHRISTMAS"**.

She then asked Noella if she
understood what that meant.

Noella thought for a minute and then finally said
"I think it is about
doing things together and
having fun with each other."

She asked if that was correct and her gramma
nodded and gave her a **HUGE HUG.**

Just as they were in sight of her gramma's house Noella felt something on her face. She looked up and watched the snowflakes fall. She reached up and started grabbing for the snowflakes. Noella twirled around. She was laughing, giggling and had a huge smile on her face. She was truly happy!

Her gramma smiled and said "Noella, I think you have now found the Spirit of Christmas. It is not about presents; it is about snowflakes, laughter, singing and happiness with people old and new."

Noella gave her gramma a big hug,
softly touched her cheek to move a
snowflake off of it and said,

"Thank you gramma.
I love you.
I have found the

SPIRIT of **CHRISTMAS**
in our

WINTER WONDERLAND.

Christmas is a favourite time of year for many.

It is definitely my happiest time of the year.

Christmas means different things to everyone but for most it probably means a special time with family and friends.

The idea for this book came about after Christmas last year. I was a little sad to be taking down the Christmas decorations until I realized that the 'Spirit of Christmas' can be enjoyed all the time as long as you are aware of what makes Christmas so special.

This book is dedicated to all who have or would like to know the meaning of Christmas.

I hope you are 'Enjoying the Spirit of Christmas' as you read this together with your children, family and friends.

Diane Gordon Yee

Look for other children's books by Diane Gordon Yee

- 2 Pillows and a Dragon
- Sweet Dreams, Sleep Tight
- Dear Santa, What should I give my Mommy for Christmas?
- A Journey of Holiday Celebrations
- Our Mouse

Copyright ©2023 by Diane Gordon Yee.
All rights reserved. No part of this publication may be reproduced, stored in a retrieval system or transmitted in any form or by any means, electronic, mechanical, photocopying, recording or otherwise, without prior written permission.
Written by Diane Gordon Yee.

www.ingramcontent.com/pod-product-compliance
Lightning Source LLC
Chambersburg PA
CBHW061155010526
44118CB00027B/2987